The Lost Wisdom

by

Ramses Khan

DORRANCE
PUBLISHING CO
EST. 1920
PITTSBURGH, PENNSYLVANIA 15238

Dorrance Publishing Co
585 Alpha Drive
Suite 103
Pittsburgh, PA 15238
Visit our website at *www.dorrancebookstore.com*

ISBN: 978-1-6393-7449-6
eISBN: 978-1-6393-7510-3

Dedicated to free-minded people everywhere

Table of Contents

vi

INTRODUCTIONS

My aim in writing this book was to challenge the imagination, to relax the mind, to give beauty and harmony to the emotions, and most of all, to give variety.

Thank you,
Rameses K. Khan

THE GENESIS OF THE MIND

Was this all in one atom of life
That exploded over eons of time
The energy made the sun
And the friction made the light
Could I be wrong or could I be right

The gasses some being water
And some being air
What causes this cosmic Explosion
What purpose in Design
Could this be the Genesis of the mind

And the nine planets
Representing the nine levels of consciousness
Before the Birth of the Beginning
The baby is born the idea of
how we got here

THE SONG OF FREEDOM

I heard the song of wisdom
Being played from the harp of my soul
Shall I tell you of something more
precious than gold

But first I must have peace
I must have your full concentration
Your humility without explanation

Then she kissed me
And my eyes opened to common sense
She whispered, "Be kind and kindness
will come to
your defense."

All life is one
And interrelated
Everything is simple not complicated.

The fools laugh
But the wise listen to my voice
Now you too, have the choice

Heaven or hell
All begins with you
Fools are many, the wise are few.

All the physical things
Will come to pass
It's only the unseen that will last.

Peace mankind
Use your imagination a
Wisdom has sang her song
of inspiration.

UNIVERSAL HARMONY

I am tuned in with universal harmony
and the peaceful rhythm flows emanating
from the divine arrangement.

Everything knows its place and song as
she moves in oneness reflecting the source.

The audience is waiting, waiting for the
mistake when there is none in the world
of perfection.

As she whispers in my soul peace,
peace be unto you,
balance and reflection is yours;

The movement is so smooth we hardly realize
we are moving.

THE LAST SCRIPTURE

The last scripture has been revealed, although they
tried to conceal, God's plan is greater.

The sun is rising in the East in order to enlighten
the deceased, time is changing the scales.

The last Scripture will let you see who we once
were and what we should be. Time is pointing at us.

Change is coming to what we once knew we should be
rejoicing to give you a little cue. The last
SCRIPTURE HAS BEEN REVEALED

UNIVERSAL PRINCIPLE

The Movement of Our Ideas
Makes the Necessary Changes

The Evolution of Our Consciousness
Demands the Struggles and Lessons of Life

Progress Depends on Death
And Time Reflects the Changes

Fear is only the Child of Ignorance
Knowledge Brings Freedom

The Cycle of Darkness and Light
is Universal Principal

FEAR

Oh, Man, limited to fear the invisible chain of
limitation holds us to the gravity of pettiness.

What is beyond the stars? What great secrets
lie on a higher plane that will make us one with
immortality?

If we could travel in the vehicle of imagination
transcending our earthly egos, we could be free
to kiss the divine.

Tuning in with other Universes that have learned
the lesson of lessons and waits for us to free
ourselves.

THE EVOLUTION OF UNITY

Listen to the sweet music of life as she plays
the tune of unity, watch the motion of nature
making perfection its destiny.

Freedom smiles at our slavery, and heaven is
amazed at our pride, when the lesson of divine
peace is right at our side.

The evolution of unity is expressing itself in
every way, but man the only slave in the universe,
holds fast to his Hell, come what may.

THE PRESENT IS THE BALANCE

The past is gone, the future in the making, now is the time for awakening.

The present is the balance, look what we could be missing, the fullness we could be kissing.

We must concentrate the power, to capture the depth, magnifying the impact the unity kept.

PART OF DIVINE

The lovely flowers touch my soul with her colors
and shape the blessed wind so cool and strong,
I hear the inspiration of a bird singing nature's
song.

The glorious light of the sun revealing the
splendor of God and always true in word, a
magnificent universe; How could this have
occurred?

And to be a part of divine and to know that
death does not exist only changing form over
and over again until we come back where it all
began.

THE GREATEST FINDING

DIG, DIG, DIG, into the tomb of self we may find
the greatest secret the past has left,

The unlimited reservoir hidden in the depths of
the soul just waiting for one fascination to
behold,

The priceless jewels of talents and nature's gifts
just the thought makes my spirits lift,

Now I am here, there's the well of greatness that
all great men drink from, there's the tree of
confidence, this is where I belong,

The greatest finding is the finding of self, the
source of happiness and the beginning of true
wealth.

Ramses

OH, HOLLYWOOD

Oh, Hollywood
I Will Not Forgive You
For Giving The World Your Eyes
And Laughing At Their Ignorance in Disguise

For Boasting Of Your Power
To Set The Pace of The World
To Have Nations Bowing At Your Feet
Lusting For Your Wealth, And Burning In Your Heat

I Charge You, Oh, Hollywood
With Corrupting Kings and Queens
And Making Sex A God Under Your Control
For Killing Creativity And Buying The Soul

I Expose You
To The World Of The Future
To Protect The Innocent One
For The Fall Of Your World Has Just Begun

THE FLOWERS OF TOMORROW

Oh, Beautiful Youth
Sent to us from Nature's Perfection
We Mold You Under Our Protection

We Dare Not Devalue
Our Flowers of Tomorrow
Less the Future Be in Shame and Sorrow

Our Corrections Are only a Reflection
Of our Undying Love
Less We Lead you Astray and be Blamed From Above

We Wish Only
That you be given the Chance to Express
The Voice of the Future at its Very Best

HUMILITY

Humility is Magnetic
Drawing the jewels of wisdom
And mirroring an eternal understanding

In meekness the prophets walked
Attracting the positive force
And universal energies visit their humility
Leaving the gifts of insight
And the wisdom of the supreme teaching
Accelerating their souls unto weightlessness freedom

Humility is releasing the ego
Freeing the vision of self
And rising above pettiness

To see through the eye of divine
Feeling the warmth of oneness
And drinking the waters of immorality

WE HAVE NOT REACHED THE LEVEL OF NATURE

We have not reached the level of nature.
Does nature kill for sport?
Does nature lie?
Does nature heal us for money?

We have not reached the level of nature.
Does nature give to receive?
Does nature take back her blessing?
Does nature hold us back when we are wrong?

We have not reached the level of nature.
Does nature give to one and not to all!
Does nature give warning first?
Does nature ever complain of man?

We have not reached the level of nature.
We think we are greater than nature.
But who will last the longest.
And who is the father and mother?

FREEDOM

Almighty God is the foundation of freedom
We must free ourselves first
The world will automatically free us

The real enemy is traditional thinking
We need a new vision
Centered on reality

Hatred denotes defeat
Passiveness means lot of hope
The balance is the key

Unity is the power of God
Division is the power of Satan
Study the ant

Stop reacting to life
We haven't used the greatest gift
Reason the intention

The price of freedom is high
But the rewards are worthy of the pain
We have not lived until we are free

RAMSES

My soul couldn't rest
When I looked in the tombs of Ramses
He begged me to take his name
and Recapture his fame

Go and build, build, build
his spirit entered mine
I knew this was a blessing from the past
As I looked into the solid gold mask

My soul lived in Egypt
Instinctively I always knew
But time is the best master
to soon would have been disaster

NEFERTITI

Nature has released its perfect jewel
And time painted the Masterpiece
That will capture the world fascination forever

Her inner beauty
Balance with her outer
Reflecting divine simplicity

Moving with the rhythm of the universe
Enslaving the beholder
Until she let them go

Queen of the east
And the mother of kindness
Nefertiti the beautiful one has come

CHECK AND BALANCES

Check and balances
The ultimate slavery
We sacrifice the harvest to Satan
In the name of Bravery

Selfishness blinds the vision
And makes us a tool
We can't see that which checks us
Making us a perfect fool

Where does it all end
And who designed this masterful scheme
How can we free ourselves
From this Satanic Beam

THE THREE WISE MEN

We lost our universal consciousness when we partook
of the forbidden tree. Now made to work by the
sweat of our mistakes.

But time sent us the three wise men who brought the
gifts of knowledge and thus we became a living soul.

The rejected is ready to fit not as the bottom rail
but as the top.

Our suffering, denoting our greatness sharpens us
for the mission.

SIMPLICITY

The voice of the universe speaks simplicity
But we seem to be attracted to the mysteries

Fear is treated as a God
And confusion is our master

We should simplify life
And emulate the basics

Genius is common sense
And progress is coming back to the basics

Confusion is Satan's intro
and mysteries his throne

If we would be simple
We would be peaceful like the universe

And being peaceful
We could receive the divine

THE SOUL

I am timeless

And carry the record of life
Who am I

I hold the balances
Of heaven and hell
Who am I

I am your soul
The life and spirit
That's who I am

You can fool the world
And even yourself
But I won't let you rest until you please me

I hold the knowledge
Of your beginning and ending
And the key to your success

So do not forget me
And I won't forget you
When old man death frees us both

BETTER TO GIVE THAN RECEIVE

I meet an empty soul, as we poured the waters of understanding, he bloomed like the flowers of spring.

It was a great pleasure watching the power of divine benefiting the giver more than the receiver.

His eyes sparkle like the reflection of the sun on the water and time was unimportant.

His tears disappeared at the presence of the sun of knowledge and he was free to enjoy the day.

Most surely it's greater to give than to receive.

LIVING MIRACLES

The greatest miracle of life
Is life itself
We are the living miracles

From sperm and ovum
To flesh and blood
Then to our personalities

How can there be doubt
Everything's already proven
We should just accept

Can we prove to ourselves
We worthy of him
Who gave us this Living Miracle

A MOMENT OF TRUTH

A moment of simplicity, a break in the hassle, a
time to observe motion, a balancing situation.

Course of success, vibes of love surround me and
make me positive just a moment of truth.

I must win, so important for myself, who is 30
million, 30 million me's in this negative situation.

My only hope 30 million hopes but I must win first
speaking for me and myself, which adds up to I alone.

So much to be gained and so nothing to be lost—
a moment of simplicity, a moment of truth.

WE ARE ONE

All life is needed
All things are necessary
We are one

The earth is a paradise
The heavens express the divine
I love all creations

What we are looking for is looking for us

We have no limitations
When we discover this we will all be free

CITY OF UNITY

The angels of paradise call us
but we listen to the demons

Divine love lower its wings to us
but we choose the vehicle of eaten

The fountain of power is at our disposal
but we love the waters of envy and jealousy

Faith calls us to the garden of bliss
but we like the blindness of confusion

God's arms are always open, we choose to look back

The gates of heaven are open to us
but we feel comfortable in hell

The eternal City Of Unity calls us
but we choose the demons of suspicion

We want the reward, but we don't want to
pay the price!

THE SAGE

Oh, Sage, where is the power to free ourselves
the power is within

Oh, Sage, what is this power, how can we use it
unity, we should sacrifice our differences for
the common good of all

Oh, Sage, how did we get in this condition
our unity was broken

Oh, Sage, how can we get our unity back
by realizing that we are one being
when you do it to one, you do it all

Oh, Sage, when we unite, what then is our next step
we should then address our needs

Oh, Sage, what then is the last step
observe and follow the laws of God in the
creation and in the Holy Scripture

THE MIND

Beloved, thinking is an art
we have to think our way to heaven
as your brother and friend
to keep this wisdom would be a sin

The mind is the reality that will truly set us free
we have to liberate ourselves from this mental death

What has killed our mind
beloved, negativity is the enemy, I find
fear, doubt, and suspicion are the ugly signs

Beloved, man is mind
The mind is in the image of divine
the flesh is the slave

One will lead us to darkness
one will lead us to the light
balance is the key
if we do it right

OPPRESSION

Beloved, when one part of humanity is oppressed
the whole body suffers
if we don't cut the rotten spot off the apple
we will lose the apple

Oppression is not necessary
God created enough for all
Jesus fed the poor and blessed the weak

God didn't create poverty
that's Satan's invention

Beloved, when one suffers all

The human family is one family
Jesus condemned the oppressor

Oh, human family, the only power the oppressor
has is the power we give him

WE NEED THE CONTROL BACK

Beloved, whoever makes your decisions
control you
We Need The Control Back

Beloved, if we allow others to think for us
we will always be a slave
We Need The Control Back

Beloved, if we don't use our mind
we will lose it
We Need The Control Back

We have the same thing they have
We Need The Control Back

Let's stop disrespecting our uniqueness
We Need The Control Back

Let's form our own brain
We Need The Control Back

Beloved, the greatest thing we can be
Be Yourself

SAVAGES DON'T BUILD PYRAMIDS

Beloved, Savages won't Build Pyramids
for your information, Africa had the first
civilization

The worth of any people is the respect they
have for themselves
If they lose that, they are headed for a certain death

Do people hate us because of the color of our skin
Is this the reason they refuse to be our friend

No, Beloved, they hate us because we first hate ourselves
when you lose self-respect there is nothing left

Beloved, remember, Savages Don't Build Pyramids
and for your information Africa had the first civilization

TRUE TRINITY

Before the beginning the mind was
the mind conceived the beginning in the form of the
idea, then the word took the idea from the spiritual world
to the world of expression

The Mind-The-Idea-The Word

The mind produces the energy
the energy takes the form of the idea
the word is the same as the prophet

The prophet takes the word
which contains the energy
that liberates the mind

WE WERE NEVER BROKEN

Beloved, we were never broken
it was never spoken
but We Were Never Broken

God always left somebody with the key
to unlock the chain and set us free
We Were Never Broken

Each one brought in a new day
they kept the light burning to show us the way
We Were Never Broken

There were male and female to carry the heavy load
somebody was always there to show us the road
We Were Never Broken

If God didn't have a place for us in his Glory
I wouldn't be here to tell the story
Beloved, We Were Never Broken

SATAN'S MAGICIANS ARE THE POLITICIANS

The Sleeping Pill of Promise is
administered to the dumb cattle
and they go back to sleep for another four years

The vehicle of politics invented
to hide Satan's ugly face.
Satan's Magician, The Politicians
his hidden ace

Nothing will ever change
which is the name of the game
we have to change
to expose Satan's blame

Satan's Magicians Are The Politicians

IT'S ONLY A CHALLENGE

It's Only A Challenge, beloved
when God wants to elevate a people
He first challenges that people

The challenge purifies them
Egypt only purified the Hebrews
Slavery only made Joseph great
and put him over the store houses

God will never put more on us
than we can bear
It's Only A Challenge, beloved

God's blessing was always on us
even when we were in the dust

Slavery took us from a piece of coal and
made us into a precious diamond

It's Only A Challenge
It's Only A Challenge

Heaven is only an hour away
that's why I am here to say
Beloved, It's Only A Challenge

WE NEED TO BE BORN AGAIN

Our Spiritual Adam
was put in a deep sleep
Our spiritual Sampson suffered a great defeat

The Christ nature was crucified on the cross
the spiritual man suffered a great loss

But God sent us the prophets
to liberate the spiritual man
only through him can humanity gain
the upper hand

We need a moral revolution
that's the only solution
We Need To Be Born Again
We Need To Be Born Again

Harmony of being
mind, body, and soul
The prophets represent balance
this should be our goal

Adam was awakened, Sampson got his
strength back, and Christ has ascended
We Need To Be Born Again

WE NEED TO RETURN TO THE INTELLECTUAL CITY

Beloved, We Need To Return To The Intellectual City
We were pointed to the valley of death

Beloved, we need be the master and not the slave
we need command and not to behave

We Need To Return To The Intellectual City
where there is no sorrow or blame
no worry of shame

Beloved, we were pointed to the valley of death
there we lost the knowledge of self

There everything will be given that we lack
if we just turn toward the City
our power will come back

Beloved, we were tricked by people
who wanted that wonderful City
but we were the first there
ain't that a pity

Beloved, there are things there beyond imagination
new worlds with no explanation
beloved, eternal death is not our goal
but to enter that wonderful City
we need to be bold
Beloved, We Need To Return To The Intellectual City

ANGEL OF INSPIRATION

Oh, agent of divine mind
Angel of Inspiration
blow your spiritual energy into our soul
Oh, spirit of life, more precious than gold

Oh, Angel Of Inspiration, pour the waters of
spiritual enlightenment on our head
before we were surely dead

We thank Allah, oh, agent of mercy
the help of prophets and kings
levels of illumination you bring

You visit us during times of prayer
in times of danger you are there

We thank Allah, we thank Allah, and we
thank Allah

Oh, Angel, visit the helpless and the oppressed
inspire us with courage
we will do our best

Oh, Angel, give us the victory over negativity

NEVER CONDEMN A WISE ONE OF SAGE

Never condemn a wise man
you may differ in point of view
beloved, that's something you should never do

They are all working for our common good
they would give their life for us if they could

Never condemn a sage

They all have different parts to play
but each one brings in a new day

beloved, never condemn a wise man

Like the body with many parts
their working together is truly an art

They are rare like precious pearls
they take us to different worlds
be it man or woman, Farakhan or W. D. Muhammad

Never Condemn A wise One of Sage

PUT THE POWER BACK

Beloved, if we take the sun
out of the universe
the worlds will be in chaos and confusion

If we take the male out of
the nation the nation is doomed

If we take God out of our nation
how can it stand

Beloved, let me inform you

If you put the Sun back in the universe
the power will come back

If you respect and support the male
the people will have a wonderful chance

If we put God back in the nation
the nation will come back into power

INVISIBLE CHAINS

Beloved, the chains are no longer on our hands
they are on our mind
that's the worst kind of slavery you can find

Can I inform you, beloved
all our mental and physical energies went to the man
ever since we have been here
but that's not my greatest fear

I need inform you
the hiding of his power is in his psychology
thar's why it's so hard to see

Lincoln and Kennedy had vision
let's put the chain on their minds
our little secret, they will never find

Beloved, all before *us* were thieves and robbers

WE KEEP THE BEAST ALIVE

Beloved, this world is built on our habitual mistakes
if we just change our behavior
this world will crumble, yes, it will tumble

May I inform you, we are the Achilles' heel
of this world

We are the foundation; if the foundation falls
then comes all

We are the secret of its power
we keep the beast alive
with our foolish Jive

Our disunity is his energy
our confusion, his enlightenment
envy of one another, his excitement

Our fears fuel him
the more we beg, the more he hardens his heart
Keeping us in hell *is* his eternal part

WE NEED CHANGE

Beloved, We Need Change
the only thing we could lose if we choose
is our poverty and mental death

We have been oppressed for so long
we think oppression is our reality
and way of life
we feel comfortable with hardship and strife

we feel right when things are going wrong
we love to hear a sad song

Beloved,
Choose life over death
be the master, not the slave
Choose a challenge over giving up
freedom over slavery
Choose light over darkness
Choose the top over the bottom
faith over fear
Choose God over the devil

Freedom is not given, it's earned

FEARFUL ONE

Oh, Fearful One
make a contribution to the struggle
you're going to die anyway
we die a little every day

Oh, Fearful One
don't let your life be in vain
release yourself from the chain

Make a contribution to the struggle
it can be small in deed, just plant the seed

You die a million deaths a day
show somebody the way

Be as bold as Minister Farakhan
who shines like the noonday sun

GOD

Beloved, God is only one
nothing can contain God
but God contains all

May I inform you
God was before the beginning
and will be after the ending

Beloved, death is inconsistent
with God's immortality

The spirit is not like the flesh
the creator is different from the creation
one is unlimited, one limited
the cause is not like the effect
one is superior, one inferior
one independent, one dependent

Beloved, God don't have to pray

God is beyond image

There is no God but God

KNOW HISTORY

A people that don't know
and study her sign
are a people that will never make progress
and will always be blind

We know the tree by the fruit it bears
when we see oppression, we know an oppressor
has to be there

If we don't want to acknowledge the facts
of our oppression, and who the oppressor is
then we don't deserve the right to be free
nor the right to live

THE PRODIGAL SON

Beloved, we have the power to change our reality
Just by using Our unity

We are pieces of each other
that need to function as one
then nothing can stop us under the sun

We are like the Prodigal Son
who made the break
The Father received him
and forgave his mistakes

PRODUCT OF DIVINE MIND

Was this all in one atom of life
That exploded over eons of time
The energy made the sun
And the friction made the light
Could I be wrong or could I be right

The gasses some being water
And *some* being air
What causes this cosmic Explosion
What purpose in Design
Could this be the product of Divine Mind

And the nine planets
Representing the nine levels of consciousness
Before the Birth of the Beginning
The baby is born the idea
How we got here

THE SONG OF WISDOM

I heard the song of wisdom
Being played from the harp of my soul
Shall I tell you of something more precious than gold

But first I must have peace
I must have your full concentration
Your humility without explanation

Then she kissed me
And my eyes opened to common sense
She whispered, "Be kind and kindness will come to
your defense."

All life is one
And inter related
Everything is simple, not complicated.

The fools laugh
But the wise listen to my voice
Now you too, have the choice.

Heaven or hell
All begins with you
Fools are many the wise are few.

All the physical things
Will come to pass
It's only the unseen that will last.

Peace mankind
Use your imagination
Wisdom has sang her song
Of inspiration.

UNIVERSAL HARMONY

I'm so tuned in with universal harmony
and the peaceful flows emanating
from the divine arrangement

Everything knows its place and song as
she moves in oneness reflecting the source.

The audience is waiting, waiting for the
mistake when there is none in the world
of perfection.

As she whispers in my soul peace,
peace be unto you,
balance and reflection is yours;

The movement is so smooth we hardly realize

we are moving.

THE LAST SCRIPTURE

The last scripture has been revealed, although they
tried to conceal, God's plan is greater.

The sun is rising in the East in order to enlighten
the deceased, time *is* changing the scales.

The last scripture will let you see who we once
were and what we should he. Time is pointing at us.

Change is coming to what we once knew we should be
rejoicing to give you a little cue. The last
SCRIPTURE HAS BEEN REVEALED.

UNIVERSAL PRINCIPLE

The Movement of Our Ideas
Makes the Necessary Changes

The Evolution of Our Consciousness
Demands the Struggles and lessons of Life

Progress Depends on Death

And Time Reflects the Changes

Fear is only the Child of Ignorance
Knowledge Brings Freedom

The Cycle of Darkness and Light
is Universal Principal

THE EVOLUTION OF UNITY

Listen to the sweet music of life as she plays
the tune of unity, watch the motion of nature
making perfection its destiny.

Freedom smiles at our slavery, and heaven is
amazed at our pride, when the lesson of divine
peace is right at our side.

The evolution of unity is expressing itself in
every way, but man the only slave in the universe,
holds fast to his Hell, come what may.

THE PRESENT IS THE BALANCE

The past is gone, the future in the making, now is the time for awakening.

The present is the balance, look what we could be missing, the fullness we could be kissing.

We must concentrate the power, to capture the Depth, magnifying the impact the unity kept

ABOUT THE AUTHOR

My aim in writing this book was to challenge the imagination, to relax the mind, to give beauty and harmony to the emotions, and most of all the variety. I am an inspired man, inspired by God.